Sancho,
the Silly Billy Goat

Miss Liz Moreno
TOLMAN

By Elizabeth Dettling Moreno

Illustrated by Mikayla Sutton

Jeremiah 29:11

Dedicated to
Lori Reyna,
who told me the story of the Billy Goat named Sancho

that her family had when she was a child.

Without her story,

I would have never created

Such a mischievous little rascal.

Most of Sancho's antics are true,

based on Mrs. Reyna's retelling.

Sancho, the silly billy goat,
Jumped in the charca and tried to stay afloat.
The chicos came running and the gallinas did, too.
Sancho was sinking--- what should they do?

"Papa, come help us!" his hijos said.
"If we can't save him, he'll soon be dead!"
So Papa brought Pepito, his burro, to the pond
To pull a rope to save his friend of which he was fond.

Pepito pulled Sancho because he knew he'd feel bad
If he lost the best goat friend he ever did have.
Before too long, the tíos and the tías, too,
Came to see what was happening at the granja zoo.

A caballero brought his lasso and swung it out just right
And caught the horns of the goat who wasn't very bright.
They all started pulling with all of their might
They'd have Sancho out before it turned night.

Sure enough, they did it, then they gave him a cold bath.

He was muy frío but he extended no wrath.

For a while, things were quiet down at the casa.

While mama made tamales using her favorite masa.

Then all of a sudden there arose quite a clatter.
"Que pasa?" Mama said, "What is the matter?"
There, on the table, just as grand as you please,
was Sancho the goat and he started to sneeze.

Now, if you've never seen it, you've missed quite a sight,
Mama grabbed her escoba and chased him left and right.
Sancho went running and tried to be incognito,
With Mama this angry, he might become cabrito!

When the niño's and niña's went to school,
Sancho thought he'd go to la escuela, too,
So he jumped on the bus and wanted to stay,
But the driver screamed and shooed him away.

He learned his lesson for a while again,
But it was almost like this critter was born just to sin.
In a few days' time, he was back to his tricks.
He grabbed a few tortillas that Mama had just fixed.

Then, before she even knew it, that billy found a bed,
He climbed in and lay down, pretending he was dead.
The chicos had been working but when they came inside,
They wondered where Sancho was and if he'd gone to hide.

Before too long, they were cansados, ready for some sleep.

That Sancho goat stayed real still and didn't make a peep.

Oh, the raucous that they made when they crawled in the covers,

After all was said and done, maybe they weren't goat lovers!

They tried again to teach him that he was just a goat,

So Papa put him in the pen and tied him with a rope.

He did the time for his latest crime, so they thought he'd learned his lesson.

But once again he pulled a stunt and it was his final messin'.

When Mama was cooking a pot of frijoles, young Sancho came around.
He climbed on top of the stove, he leaped in a single bound.
The dumb little goat burned his hoofs and then he kicked his feet,
When he got done, the beans fell down, they were not fit to eat.

Out of all the stunts the kid did do, this was one was really bad,
You never saw Mamacita so angry and raving mad!
So Sancho soon was banished, the tíos took him away.
They never said what happened to him, even to this day.

The moral of this story is meant for one and all...
Remember that silliness always goes before a fall.
And if you are a little goat, remember what I've said...
Behave yourself, stay off the stove, and out of people's beds.

Forsake the **foolish**, and live;
and go in the way of understanding.
King James Version

glossary

1. charca – (char ka) – pond
2. chicos – (chi cose) – little boys
3. gallinas – (gug yee nas) – chickens
4. hijos – (ee hose) – sons
5. tíos, tías – (tee ohs, tee uz) – uncles, aunts
6. granja – (gran ha) – farm
7. caballero – (ka bah yer oh) – cowboy
8. muy frio – (mooey free oh) – very cold
9. masa – (mah sah) – dough for tamales
10. casa – (kah sah) – house
11. tamales – (ta mah lays) – a starchy corn-based dough usually with a filling, which is steamed in a corn husk
12. "¿Que pasa?" – (kay pas ah) – What's going on?
13. escoba – (es sko bah) – broom
14. cabrito – (kah bree tow) – barbecued goat
15. niños, niñas – (neen yoes, neen yas) – little boys and girls
16. la escuela – (la es cuel lah) – the school
17. tortillas – (tor ti yas)round, thin flatbread for dining
18. cansado – (kahn sod oh) – tired
19. frijoles – (free hole lays) – cooked pinto beans
20. Mamacita – (ma ma see tah) – little mama

CPSIA information can be obtained
at www.ICGtesting.com
Printed in the USA
JSHW041400150623
43070JS00012B/51